Count Your Blessings

pil

Publications International, Ltd.

Cover photo: Shutterstock.com

Interior photos: Getty: 21, 26, 28; Shutterstock.com: 3, 7, 10, 16

Scripture quotations from *The Holy Bible, King James Version.* Copyright © 1977, 1984, Thomas Nelson, Inc., Publishers.

Louis Weber, CEO
Publications International, Ltd.
7373 North Cicero Avenue
Lincolnwood, Illinois 60712

ISBN: 978-1-68022-024-7

Manufactured in China.

8 7 6 5 4 3 2 1

Count Your Blessings

Count your blessings, name them one by one:
Count your blessings, see what God hath done.

—Johnson Oatman, Jr.

When you look around you today, know the blessing of seeing God in every smiling face. Reflect that blessing in your own eyes, silently and with a kind heart.

Blessed be the God and Father of our Lord Jesus Christ, who hath blessed us with all spiritual blessings in heavenly places in Christ.

—Ephesians 1:3

Count Your Blessings

God's Word

Lord, focusing on your Word is a great blessing. The more I keep it before me, the more faithfully I walk in your ways. Help me to make the most of every opportunity I have to read, think about, and discuss the things you share with us through the Scriptures.

And all these blessings shall come on thee, and overtake thee, if thou shalt hearken unto the voice of the Lord thy God.

—Deuteronomy 28:2

Count Your Blessings

*J*ust a tiny seed of faith, watered with love, wisdom, and hard work, grows into a majestic tree of blessings.

A faithful man shall abound with blessings.

—Proverbs 28:20

Count Your Blessings

Creation

What "speaks" to you in nature? The amazing variety of birds coming and going at your bird feeder? The petals on those wildflowers by your mailbox? The smell of the air after a rainstorm? The night sky? Maybe you simply wonder how those weeds can find a way to thrive in the cracks of the sidewalk. Whatever impresses us among the things God has made, it's a part of his messaging system to us, inviting us to search him out and find relationship with him.

There shall be showers of blessing.

—Ezekiel 34:26

Count Your Blessings

Awake each morning in gratitude for the blessing of another day, for each is a precious gift and a priceless opportunity to live, to laugh, and to love.

It is a good thing to give thanks unto the Lord, and to sing praises unto thy name, O Most High:

To shew forth thy lovingkindness in the morning, and thy faithfulness every night,

Upon an instrument of ten strings, and upon the psaltery; upon the harp with a solemn sound.

For thou, Lord, hast made me glad through thy work: I will triumph in the works of thy hands.

—Psalm 92:1–4

Count Your Blessings

Community

*L*ord, my heart is uplifted as I think of the special gift you have given me: a community of faith. I thank you for my church and for the dear people who have become part of my support system. I thank you for your invitation to spend time with you.

I thank you for the blessings you offer through church attendance: the fellowship and care of other believers; the refreshment of the words of Scripture, and the feeling as the power of prayer washes over us. I need to experience your presence, Lord, in your house, and become involved in your work.

Count Your Blessings

Jesus said that those who would believe in him without having seen him would be blessed. It is a blessing to live in such joy. People can work a lifetime to amass money and all the things it can buy without feeling such true joy. Yet those who trust in Christ have an abiding, "indescribable and glorious" joy that fills their innermost being. This doesn't mean we spend all our moments singing tra-la-la, though. It means that even on our most trying days, we land on hope instead of despair, love instead of hate, and peace instead of anxiety. Our joy in belonging to Christ—in having an eternal hope—trumps every trial.

Count Your Blessings

Family

If you ask the most accomplished people in the world what is most important to them, they will all give the same answer: family. The love and devotion of family serves as the foundation upon which dreams are built. The support of family acts as wings, which each member can use to fly to new heights of achievement. The honesty and trustworthiness of family creates a sanctuary that can be depended upon in times of struggle and discouragement. The blessings of family bolster the spirit. The pride of family gladdens the heart. With a loving family standing behind you, it becomes much easier to stand on your own.

Count Your Blessings

Daily Life

If we look hard enough, we find blessings in everything, even dirty dishes, unwashed laundry, and chocolate stains on the refrigerator door. Those things remind us that we are part of a family, for better and for worse. But mostly for better.

I will bless the Lord at all times: his praise shall continually be in my mouth.

My soul shall make her boast in the Lord: the humble shall hear thereof, and be glad.

O magnify the Lord with me, and let us exalt his name together.

—Psalm 34:1–3

Parents and Mentors

Moms are gentle enough to raise babies, strong enough to support teenagers, patient enough to help adult children when needed, and resilient enough to do it all over again when they become grandmothers. Thanks for our mothers, grandmothers, godmothers, aunts, and all those women who have been wise and loving teachers and mentors.

The dreams my mother dream for me are now all coming true: a happy home and family and work I love to do. As I look back upon my life, of one thing I am sure: For every blessing I can count, I owe so much to her.

Count Your Blessings

Dads are wonderful, because—just like us—they are kids at heart. They love silly jokes, adventure walks to gather shells or rocks, laughing at our funny drawings, and getting in on our pranks. Dads sing us to sleep on hot summer nights, tell us funny stories when we're feeling sad, and make goofy faces in the rearview mirror to keep us entertained during long trips. Thanks for our fathers, grandfathers, godfathers, uncles, and all those men in our lives who give and guide so generously.

If ye then, being evil, know how to give good gifts unto your children, how much more shall your Father which is in heaven give good things to them that ask him?

—Matthew 7:11

Friendship

A healthy friendship enhances our lives. What a blessing to have someone who wants to share all our joys and sorrows. We should continually strive to be the kind of friend God would like us to be— and the kind of friend that we would like to have.

Father, you help us to live gracefully by blessing us with wonderful friends. Thank you for making them as good as you are. Amen.

Count Your Blessings

Single Life

My God, I thank you for the blessings of the single life. One of your plans was for people to get married and have children. But I know that your good and perfect will is also for some of us to live unmarried and not have children.

For this life I thank you. For the gift to be free to learn to love without clinging. To seek relationships without owning, to offer my love and kindness among many friends.

Yes, Lord at times I am lonely, like all people can be. So I ask you to fill those times of emptiness with your presence. Enter into the barren places with your refreshing water of life.Give me peace in my daily work, joy in the pursuit of wholeness, and comfort in the solitary nights. And please continue to give me a giving heart.

Count Your Blessings

Married Life

That we found one another is a miracle. That we love one another is a blessing. That we wed and live as one is a joy that cannot be expressed, only shared in the precious experiences of each new day together.

Life looks kindly on those who love and bestows special blessings on those who join their hearts.

Count Your Blessings

New Couples

May the blessing of God fill your days. Especially, may you develop the perfect balance of duties to family and responsibilities at work and worship. As you seek serenity in these things, may you find great cause for celebration, knowing that the one who loves you unconditionally remains at the center of all your activity.

Wherefore they are no more twain, but one flesh. What therefore God hath joined together, let not man put asunder.

—Matthew 19:6

Count Your Blessings

The Children
in Our Lives

All I don't know, Lord, is most apparent when children are around. Their curiosity is insatiable. I'm grateful I don't need all the answers, just a willingness to consider the questions and honor the questioners. Knock, seek, and ask are imperative verbs implying your blessing on our quests.

Suffer little children to come unto me, and forbid them not: for of such is the kingdom of God.

—Luke 18:16

Count Your Blessings

Encourage your child to learn, to master, to question—to try. It may feel like a big adventure and maybe even a huge risk, but you can relax, knowing that God is blessing the undertaking and providing the fuel for the journey.

For I will pour water upon him that is thirsty, and floods upon the dry ground: I will pour my spirit upon thy seed, and my blessing upon thine offspring.

—Isaiah 44:3

Our Talents and Abilities

All our opportunities, abilities, and resources come from God. They are given to us to hold in sacred trust for him. Cooperating with God will permit us to generously pass on to others some of the many blessings from his rich storehouse.

As every man hath received the gift, even so minister the same one to another, as good stewards of the manifold grace of God.

—1 Peter 4:10

Count Your Blessings

Work

What a blessing, Almighty One, to be able to earn a living for the family! To be free of worry about what they will eat, or what they will wear, or where they will sleep. You have given us so much: house, flowers, table and chairs, even cameras and smartphones to help us remember these days that are flying by. And your gifts are a serious calling: Show us how to give in return!

Blessed is every one that feareth the Lord; that walketh in his ways.

For thou shalt eat the labour of thine hands: happy shalt thou be, and it shall be well with thee.

—Psalm 128:1–2

Opening Our Eyes

It sometimes takes a tragic event to open our eyes to the blessings that surround us, to show us the joy in life's simple moments. Day-to-day activities and events can seem mundane and repetitive until something happens that shakes our foundation and brings into sharp focus what is truly important and precious. Our family, friends, our neighbors, and our communities suddenly become havens of love, support, and comfort in the midst of tragedy.

Wise is the person who can see the magic and wonder in simple things without having to suffer a great loss or disaster. Happy is the person who knows that life's greatest treasures are often buried deep within the simplest things, waiting to be discovered by those who are paying attention.

Count Your Blessings

There shall be showers of blessing,

This is the promise of love;

There shall be seasons refreshing,

Sent from the Savior above.

Showers of blessing,

Showers of blessing we need;

Mercy drops around us are falling,

But for the showers we plead.

There shall be showers of blessing,

Precious reviving again;

Over the hills and the valleys

Sound of abundance of rain.

—Major Daniel W. Whittle

Count Your Blessings

In Times of Difficulty

*L*ord, it's hard to count your blessings when all around me is chaos and despair. Though my heart is heavy and my mind cluttered, please help me to realize that before a flower can show its beauty to the sun, it first is a seed buried in the dirt. Help me to stand above the negative things in life and cast my eyes instead  upon the positives that are always there, like the seedling, growing toward the moment when it will appear above ground, turning its face to the sun.

Count Your Blessings

Salvation belongeth unto the Lord: thy blessing is upon thy people.

—Psalm 3:8

Comes the Light

From the dark night of the soul
Comes the blessing of the dawn.
From the deep wounds of the heart
Comes the gift of love reborn.
From the chaos of confusion
Comes the calm of clarity.
From the anguish of discord
Comes the peace of harmony.
From the grieving of great loss
Comes the happiness of new life.
From the coldness of despair
Comes the warmth of our Father's light.

New Beginnings

What a blessing to have a second chance! Grant me the wisdom to use this opportunity wisely. And save me from the fear that I'll fall into the same old traps as last time. This is a brand new day, a whole new beginning. Fantastic!

And let the beauty of the Lord our God be upon us: and establish thou the work of our hands upon us; yea, the work of our hands establish thou it.

—Psalm 90:17

28

Count Your Blessings

Lord, how grateful I am that you are willing to go before me to prepare the way. Even when I sense that a new opportunity is from you and has your blessing, I've learned I still need to stop and ask you to lead before I take the first step. Otherwise I will stumble along in the dark tripping over stones of my own creation! Everything goes more smoothly when you are involved, Lord.

He that hath clean hands, and a pure heart; who hath not lifted up his soul unto vanity, nor sworn deceitfully. He shall receive the blessing from the Lord, and righteousness from the God of his salvation.

—Psalm 24:4–5

Count Your Blessings

*B*lessing, and glory, and wisdom, and thanksgiving, and honour, and power, and might, be unto our God for ever and ever. Amen.

—Revelation 7:12

*N*ight and day may we give you praise and thanks, because you have shown us that all things belong to you, and all blessings are gifts from you.

—Clement of Alexandria